Christopher Columbus

History Maker Bios

Susan Bivin Aller

LERNER PUBLICATIONS COMPANY • MINNEAPOLIS

For Carl Robert, whose voyage is just beginning

Map on p. 45 by Laura Westlund
Illustrations by Tim Parlin

Text copyright © 2003 by Susan Bivin Aller
Illustrations copyright © 2003 by Lerner Publications Company

Lerner Publications Company
A division of Lerner Publishing Group
241 First Avenue North
Minneapolis, MN 55401 U.S.A.

Website address: www.lernerbooks.com

Library of Congress Cataloging-in-Publication Data

Aller, Susan Bivin.
    Christopher Columbus / by Susan Bivin Aller.
        p.   cm. — (History maker bios)
    Summary: Introduces the life of explorer Christopher Columbus, the first man known to cross the Atlantic Ocean, and discusses what he found when he reached the islands now known as the West Indies.
    Includes bibliographical references and index.
    ISBN: 0–8225–0398–0 (lib. bdg. : alk. paper)
    1. Columbus, Christopher—Juvenile literature. 2. Explorers—America—Biography—Juvenile literature. 3. Explorers—Spain—Biography—Juvenile literature. 4. America—Discovery and exploration—Spanish—Juvenile literature. [1. Columbus, Christopher. 2. Explorers. 3. America—Discovery and exploration—Spanish.] I. Title. II. Series.
E111 .A4 2003
970.01'5'092—dc21   2002000944

Manufactured in the United States of America
2 3 4 5 6 – JR – 08 07 06 05 04

TABLE OF CONTENTS

INTRODUCTION

In 1492 Christopher Columbus left Spain with ninety men aboard three sailing ships. He had a grand dream. His dream was to be the first person to reach Asia by sailing around the world across the Atlantic Ocean.

Columbus made it to the other side of the ocean. He thought the islands he found there were near Asia. But he was wrong. They were near a continent that was not on any map. It was America.

Columbus brought Europeans and Americans together for the first time. He opened the route to the Americas for other explorers. And the world was never the same again.

This is his story.

1 THE BOY WHO LOVED THE SEA

A red-haired boy gripped the rail of a small ship as it moved away from shore. His gray eyes searched the sparkling water ahead. Above him, a great sail filled with wind. The creaking ship gained speed. Salt water sprayed the boy's ruddy cheeks.

He looked back at Genoa. The city was spread out along a narrow strip of land between the sea and mountains. Merchant ships crowded the docks. Sun gleamed on the domes of churches. The boy could just make out the area where his family and the other weavers lived.

Christopher grew up in the exciting seaport of Genoa, Italy.

TRADE WITH THE INDIES

In Columbus's time, Arab traders brought silks, spices, and gold from the Indies. Italian merchants in port cities like Genoa bought all the traders' goods. Then the Italians sold the goods for higher prices to people in other European countries. Merchants from the other countries wanted to go directly to the Indies. Then they wouldn't have to deal with Arab traders or Italian merchants.

The boy's name was Christopher Columbus. He was born in Genoa, Italy, in 1451. The thrill of his first sailing trip made him want to spend his whole life with ships and the sea. He certainly didn't want to be a weaver like his father and grandfathers.

Every day, ships unloaded spices, silks, tea, and jewels from Asia onto the Genoa docks. They took Italian wool, linen, armor, copper, and tin to sell in far-off lands. The merchants of Genoa grew rich.

Christopher loved the sea. In 1476, when he was twenty-five, he sailed north with a fleet of five Italian ships. A merchant had probably hired him to take wool to a customer. Suddenly, off the coast of Portugal, pirates attacked the ships. Three of the ships sank. Many sailors died. Christopher was wounded. He nearly lost his life. But he held on to an oar and swam six miles to the shore of Portugal.

Pirates often attacked merchant ships off the coast of Portugal.

How lucky for Christopher! Portugal was the world's best place for learning about the sea. Scholars and sea captains from many countries were in Portugal. They designed ships that could stay at sea for several weeks without needing to stop for fresh supplies. They made new instruments for guiding ships through uncharted waters.

No one painted a picture of Christopher while he was alive, so no one knows what he looked like. He may have looked like this.

Christopher and Bartholomew drew maps like this map of the world. It shows what Europeans had discovered by the mid-1400s.

Many merchants and seamen from Genoa lived in Lisbon, Portugal. One of them was Christopher's younger brother, Bartholomew. The brothers went into business together, making and selling maps. Every time the Portuguese found a new island or explored more of the coast of Africa, Christopher and his brother added these places to their maps.

2 A WILD IDEA

Christopher's favorite book was *The Travels of Marco Polo.* Two hundred years earlier, Marco Polo had traveled from Italy to the Indies. Europeans called India, China, and Japan the Indies. Christopher read Marco Polo's stories about spices, jewels, and houses covered with gold. He wanted to go to China and bring back these treasures for himself.

But by the mid-1400s, Turkish warriors blocked the route between Europe and the Indies. They wouldn't let Europeans through. Traders were trying to find a way around the Turks to get to the treasure of the Indies.

Christopher heard about another way that no one had tried. It was to sail around the world to the Indies by going west across the Atlantic Ocean.

Christopher read about Marco Polo and his journeys to the Indies.

For centuries, people had thought the world was flat. But by Christopher's time, most educated people knew the world was round. They thought it was covered by water, except for one large landmass of Europe and Asia and Africa. Christopher was sure that when he had sailed to the other side of the Atlantic Ocean he would be in the Indies. He wanted to be the first person to make the journey.

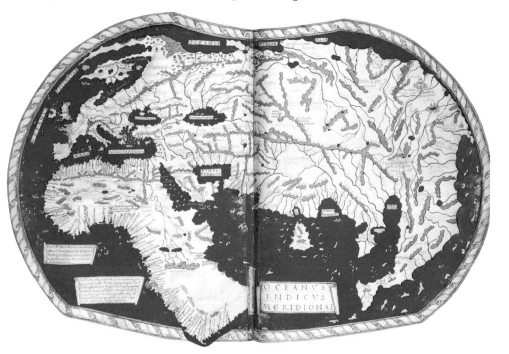

By 1489 Europeans had mapped much of Europe, Africa, and Asia. They didn't know that other continents existed.

THE VIKING EXPLORERS

Hundreds of years before Columbus, Vikings sailed from Norway across the Atlantic Ocean. Their small ships could not sail many days without stopping for supplies. Luckily they found islands, like stepping stones, across the North Atlantic. There they could stay awhile, build settlements, and then explore farther. First they settled in Iceland. Then they went to Greenland and Newfoundland. In about the year 1000, the Vikings reached the coast of what is now New England. No one kept written records of these voyages. So by Columbus's time, Europeans had forgotten all about the Viking explorers.

Christopher sailed along the coast of Africa and north to Iceland in ships like these.

In the next few years, Christopher sailed on many merchant ships. He learned about ocean winds and currents. He sailed as far north as Iceland. And he went south along the coast of Africa. He sailed out into the Atlantic Ocean to the Azores and the Canary Islands.

Christopher married a rich Portuguese woman named Felipa. They had a son called Diego. Felipa's family let Christopher use their library to study astronomy and geography and math. He was lucky, because books were very rare. But he made a lot of mistakes when he taught himself astronomy and geography and math. He thought the world was much, much smaller than it really was.

Christopher studied astronomy and geography and math.

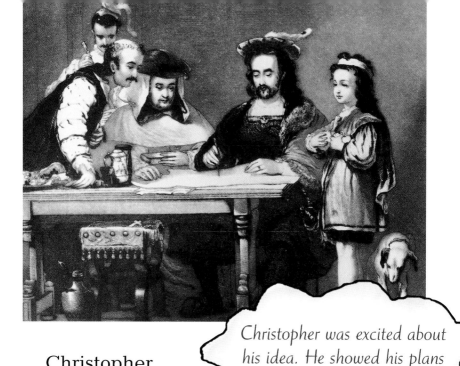

Christopher boasted that he could certainly sail around the world to the Indies. He just needed someone to pay for the ships, supplies, and crew. And when he succeeded, he would bring back riches for all who helped.

Christopher was excited about his idea. He showed his plans to many people.

He asked King John of Portugal for money. The king wanted treasure as much as any other king. But his ships were trying to reach the Indies by sailing around the southern tip of Africa. He couldn't afford to waste money on Columbus's wild idea.

Next, Columbus went to Spain. He asked King Ferdinand and Queen Isabella for money. The queen liked Columbus and his grand idea. But she had no money to spare. Spain was fighting a war against the Moors, and it was costing a lot of money.

If Columbus really found a new way to the Indies, Spain would become rich and powerful. But the queen's advisers told her Columbus's idea would never work. She didn't dare risk her money. So Spain refused Columbus, too.

Columbus told King Ferdinand and Queen Isabella about his idea. He wanted their help.

Even so, Columbus decided to stay near the Spanish court and promote his plan. He was a big talker and a good salesman. Some people thought he was brilliant. They wanted to give him the money. Some thought he was crazy.

In January 1492, Ferdinand and Isabella won the war against the Moors. But Columbus had grown tired of waiting. On the day of the victory celebration, he rode away from the city on a mule. The next day, a royal messenger galloped up behind him. He told Columbus to come back. The king and queen had changed their minds.

3 SAILING THE OCEAN BLUE

Columbus told Ferdinand and Isabella that he would claim all the lands he found for Spain. The more land Spain owned, the richer and more powerful it would become. The king and queen liked that idea.

Columbus bids farewell to Isabella. He is ready to board the SANTA MARIA.

In return, they would make him the Admiral of the Ocean Seas. They would give Columbus and his family ten percent of all the money they made from the new countries.

Columbus took three months to get ready. He would command a fleet of three wooden ships—the *Niña, Pinta,* and *Santa Maria.* Columbus would sail in the *Santa Maria.* On August 3, 1492, the ships sailed from the Spanish city of Palos.

The three ships carried a total of ninety men. The sailors slept on deck, among the ship's ropes, sails, and other equipment. In bad weather, the crew found shelter in the hold, along with rats and stinking water that leaked into the ship. There was only one cabin on the *Santa Maria,* and it was for Columbus. The men cooked on deck over fires built in boxes filled with sand. They ate salted meats and fish, dried peas and beans, onions and garlic, and hard, dry ship's biscuits. They caught fish from the ocean. When fresh water was scarce, the crew drank wine instead.

The SANTA MARIA sails out in front of the NIÑA and the PINTA.

Columbus headed for the Canary Islands. He knew about steady winds there that would blow his ships in the right direction. After the Canaries, they entered waters no one had ever sailed before. Columbus knew the crew would be frightened if he told them how far they had sailed from home. So he lied and gave them false distances.

Columbus probably drew this picture of a Spanish ship at sea.

Sailors were afraid there might be sea serpents lurking in unknown waters.

One day the winds stopped. The ships drifted through what looked like a sea of grass. The sailors were terrified. They expected monsters to come out of the grass and eat them.

At last the sails filled with wind. The ships moved out into the open water. And the men breathed sighs of relief.

More days passed. Then a shout went up from a sailor on the *Niña.* "Land!" But it was only low clouds in the distance.

WHO SAW LAND FIRST?

Ferdinand and Isabella offered a reward to the person who first saw land. It should have been given to a sailor on the *Pinta* named Rodrigo. But Columbus claimed the reward for himself. He said he had seen a light on land the night before. No one dared to argue with him.

Day after day, for two more weeks, they sailed on. The sailors were truly afraid. Would they ever see land again? Columbus must be mad! The sailors planned to take control of the *Santa Maria*, push Columbus overboard, and turn the ships around. But Columbus was a strong leader. He promised that if they didn't reach land in three more days, he would turn back. The ships continued westward.

On the first day, a strong wind blew the ships faster. On the second day, sticks and branches floated by. Birds landed in the ropes. The smell of flowers filled the air.

Early on the third morning, a sailor perched high in the rigging of the *Pinta* called out "Land! Land!" The *Pinta* fired a cannon to tell the other ships. This time the land was real. Columbus's luck had held.

The men saw a white beach shining in the faint dawn light. They gave thanks to God. They rowed Columbus to shore in his ship's boat. With the banner of Queen Isabella held high, Columbus claimed the land for Spain. It was October 12, 1492.

Columbus comes ashore and claims the land for Spain.

4 THE NEW WORLD

The people who lived on the island gathered as Columbus and his men stepped on shore. The islanders were tall, brown skinned, and naked, with straight black hair. They pointed to the sky and to the great white sails of the three ships anchored in their harbor. Maybe they thought that Columbus and his men had dropped from the heavens.

Columbus looked at the smiling, excited people. He had reached the Indies at last! He would call these people Indians.

Columbus made signs of friendship. He offered the Indians glass beads, little bells, and red caps. In return, they gave him gifts of cotton thread and brightly colored parrots.

Some of the Indians wore gold rings in their ears and noses. Columbus wondered where the gold came from. He would make the Indians take him to where he could get more, much more.

The people who live on the island watch Columbus and his men land on the beach.

Each day Columbus wrote reports for the king and queen. He described the gentle people he had found. The Indians were generous. They shared everything they had. He would teach them to wear clothes, he wrote. He would make them into Christians, and he would bring some of them back to Spain with him. He thought they would make good slaves.

WHAT THEY FOUND

Columbus and the explorers who came after him found many things in the Americas that were new to them. They had never tasted chocolate. They had never eaten pineapples, potatoes, tomatoes, or corn. They had never seen people smoke tobacco. And they had never slept in hammocks. But they soon discovered that hammocks made great beds for sailors on ships!

Columbus asks the Indians where he can find gold.

Columbus soon realized there was no gold on the island except the trinkets the Indians wore. They told him about a large kingdom where there was much gold. Columbus thought that the kingdom must be China. He made the Indians take him there. But it wasn't China. It was the island we call Cuba. And Columbus didn't find much gold there, either, except for tiny amounts in the beds of rivers.

By December Columbus was becoming desperate for treasure. All he had to show for his trouble so far were a few gold ornaments and a lot of parrots!

The SANTA MARIA *wrecks on the coast of the island of Hispaniola.*

Then he heard about a large island east of Cuba where the Indians had found more gold. He sailed near the island on Christmas Eve. Around midnight the pilot decided to take a nap. A ship's boy took the steering tiller.

Suddenly, the *Santa Maria* snagged on a coral reef. It shuddered to a stop. The ship began to sink. The local Indian chief sent men and canoes to carry Columbus, his men, and all the ship's supplies to safety. Columbus named the island Hispaniola in honor of Spain.

The *Pinta* had gone ahead to explore the other side of Hispaniola. So Columbus had only one ship left, the *Niña*. It was not big enough to hold all of his men.

He told thirty-nine of his men to stay on the island and build a fort. He told them to make the Indians collect gold. Then they should bury the gold under the fort for safekeeping. Columbus would take the rest of the men (and some captive Indians) back to Spain. He promised he would return with many more ships and supplies.

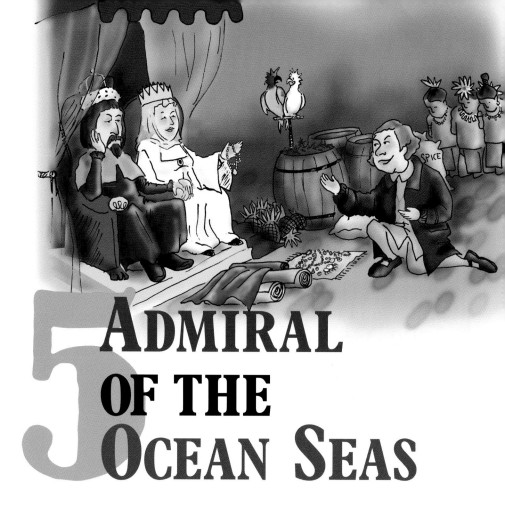

5 ADMIRAL OF THE OCEAN SEAS

On the trip back to Europe, the ship ran into a hurricane. It almost sank. Columbus feared he might not reach Spain. Then the world would never know about his amazing journey. So he wrote a quick account of his journey, put it in a barrel, and threw it overboard.

Columbus survived the difficult voyage after all. He landed at Palos, Spain. Palos gave him a hero's welcome. King Ferdinand and Queen Isabella were in Barcelona, eight hundred miles away. Columbus set out to give them his report.

Crowds of people came to watch as Columbus rode by. Behind him came six Indians wearing feathers and gold ornaments. Sailors carried cages of parrots and other gifts from the islanders.

Columbus presents gifts to Queen Isabella and King Ferdinand upon his return to Spain.

Columbus explains what he found to Isabella and Ferdinand.

Columbus had enough spices and gold to show he had found some of the riches he had promised. He presented everything to the king and queen. He told them there was a lot more where that came from.

The king and queen gave Columbus the rewards he had asked for. He told his amazing story over and over again. He made everything sound more wonderful than it really was. There was gold everywhere, he said. There were rare spices and other treasures. All he needed were more men and more ships. Then he would go back to get these treasures for Spain.

In September 1493, Columbus sailed again. This time he commanded a fleet of seventeen ships and 1,200 men. When they arrived on Hispaniola, they expected to be greeted by the men they had left behind ten months earlier. There was only silence. The fort had been burned to the ground. All the Spaniards were dead.

Columbus returned to the island of Hispaniola on his second voyage.

THE END OF THE STORY

The people who lived in the West Indies had no way to protect themselves from the Spaniards. The Spaniards had steel knives and gunpowder. They had horses, dogs, armor, and a powerful greed for gold. The Spaniards took over the land. They forced the Indians to do anything they wanted. Within a few decades of Columbus's arrival, there were almost no Indians left in the West Indies. Some had died of starvation or disease. Others had been killed by the Spaniards.

Columbus learned that the Spaniards had raided Indian villages for food and gold. They had mistreated the Indians. So the Indians had killed the Spaniards. Columbus dug for the gold his men were supposed to have buried at the fort. But there was none. Columbus moved inland, where the Indians had reported finding a small amount of gold in the ground.

He told some of his men to stay there and build a settlement. They should plant crops and make the Indians dig for gold. Then Columbus went to explore other islands. He took Indians with him to do the hard labor. When they didn't find any gold mines—and only a little gold dust in the streams—Columbus made them prisoners. He sent them to Spain on one of his ships. Slaves were not as valuable as gold, but they were worth something.

Columbus forces Indians to search for gold dust.

Some of the Spaniards who took the captive Indians to Spain told about the problems Columbus was having keeping peace in the islands. Ferdinand and Isabella wanted Columbus to explain. He returned to Spain to answer their questions in person. He boasted that he would certainly find China next time, if they would just send him out again with more ships and men. Then the treasures of the Indies would be theirs at last.

This map of Hispaniola was published with a letter Columbus wrote about his discoveries.

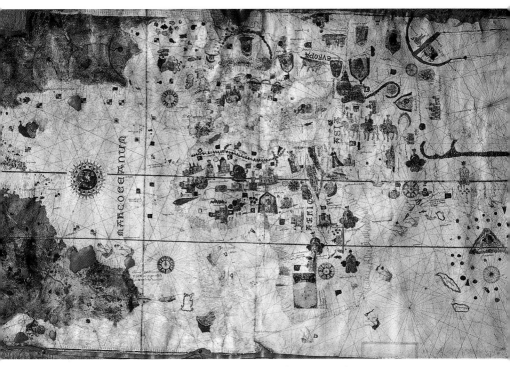

Columbus's pilot drew this map of the world.

In 1498 Columbus sailed again to the islands. Months passed, and he found very little gold for the Spanish treasury. It had taken the Indians many years to find what gold they had. Columbus's men had taken all the gold jewelry and trinkets from them, and the Indians had no way to find more. Columbus sent more Indian captives to Spain. They were all he had found that was worth anything. Many of the Indians died on the ships from disease and mistreatment.

Columbus was brought back to Spain in chains.

Columbus was failing to bring back the treasure the king and queen wanted. And the Spaniards under his command were causing much trouble in the islands. The king and queen sent an official to take charge of the islands. He arrested Christopher Columbus and sent him back to Spain in chains.

Columbus appealed to Ferdinand and Isabella. He wanted one more chance to prove that he had found the gateway to the Indies, not just a string of islands leading to nowhere.

In 1502 the king and queen granted Columbus's wish. At the age of fifty-one, the Admiral of the Ocean Seas sailed for the fourth and last time out into the Atlantic. He took his second son, thirteen-year-old Ferdinand, with him. Two years later, Columbus returned home to Spain, ill and worn out.

Until he died in 1506, Columbus insisted that he had found a short way across the Ocean Sea to the Indies explored by Marco Polo. We know the islands he explored are actually part of the Americas. They are called the West Indies.

Although Columbus failed to find what he was looking for, he succeeded in becoming the first person with enough courage and skill to sail all the way across the Atlantic Ocean to the other side. After that, more and more people sailed along the same route and settled in America. They changed the world forever.

TIMELINE

CHRISTOPHER COLUMBUS
WAS BORN IN 1451.

In the year . . .

1476   he was shipwrecked off Portugal and swam to shore.   Age 25

1477   he became a mapmaker with his brother Bartholomew.

1480   he married Felipa Perestrello.   Age 29

        his son Diego was born.

1486   he began a campaign to get money from the king and queen of Spain.

1488   his son Ferdinand was born.

1492   Spain agreed to sponsor Columbus.

        he sailed from Palos, Spain, on August 2 with three ships.

        he landed in the West Indies on October 12.   AGE 41

1493   he returned to Palos, Spain, on March 15.

        he began his second voyage in September with seventeen ships.

1498   he began his third voyage on May 30 with six ships.

1500   he was arrested and sent back to Spain in chains.

1502   he began his fourth voyage on May 11, taking thirteen-year-old Ferdinand with him.   Age 51

1504   he returned to Spain on November 7.

1506   he died in Valladolid, Spain, on May 20.   Age 55

WHERE DID COLUMBUS EXPLORE?

1ST VOYAGE: San Salvador • Bahamas • Cuba • Hispaniola

2ND VOYAGE: Guadeloupe • Nevis • St. Croix • Virgin Islands • Cuba • Jamaica

3RD VOYAGE: Trinidad • South America

4TH VOYAGE: Honduras • Nicaragua • Costa Rica • Panama

Why do we call our continent "North America" and not "North Columbia"?

An Italian navigator named Amerigo Vespucci explored the coast of South America a few years after Columbus and wrote a colorful account of his voyages. In 1507 a group of French mapmakers decided to put the name "America" on the map they designed that showed for the first time that the New World is a landmass separate from Europe and Asia.

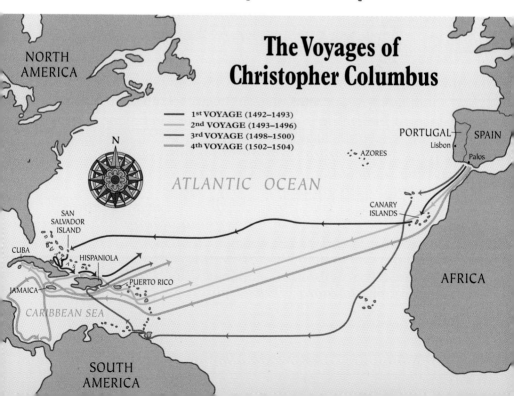

The Voyages of Christopher Columbus

NORTH AMERICA

1st VOYAGE (1492–1493)
2nd VOYAGE (1493–1496)
3rd VOYAGE (1498–1500)
4th VOYAGE (1502–1504)

N

ATLANTIC OCEAN

PORTUGAL   SPAIN
Lisbon
Palos

AZORES

CANARY ISLANDS

SAN SALVADOR ISLAND

CUBA

HISPANIOLA

PUERTO RICO

JAMAICA

CARIBBEAN SEA

AFRICA

SOUTH AMERICA

FURTHER READING

NONFICTION
De Kay, James T. *Meet Christopher Columbus.* New York: Random House, 2001. A clear and exciting retelling of Columbus's life.

Fritz, Jean. *Where Do You Think You're Going, Christopher Columbus?* New York: Putnam, 1980. A lively story about Columbus, who bravely told his sailors to go "Adelante!" until they found the New World.

Roop, Peter, and Connie Roop. *Christopher Columbus.* New York: Scholastic, 2000. This gripping story of Columbus's life is told using excerpts from his journals.

FICTION
Conrad, Pam. *Pedro's Journal.* New York: Scholastic, 1992. A ship's boy on the *Santa Maria* keeps a "diary."

Dorris, Michael. *Morning Girl.* New York: Hyperion, 1992. A Taino Indian sister and brother watch strangers land on their island in 1492.

Fischetto, Laura. *All Pigs on Deck: Christopher Columbus's Second Marvelous Voyage.* New York: Delacorte, 1991. Bright pictures show how Columbus brought pigs to the New World.

Sís, Peter. *Follow the Dream: The Story of Christopher Columbus.* New York: Knopf, 1991. This picture book shows Columbus's story with richly detailed maps, cutaway drawings, and a pictorial log.

Yolen, Jane. *Encounter.* New York: Harcourt, 1992. A Taino Indian boy tells what happened when Columbus landed on San Salvador in 1492.

WEBSITES

The Columbus Navigation Homepage
<http://www1.minn.net/~keithp/>
This detailed site examines the history, navigation, and landfall of Christopher Columbus.

What Did Columbus Look Like?
<http://commfaculty.fullerton.edu/lester/writings/admiral.html>
Nobody knows for sure, but this website will show you some interesting ideas.

SELECT BIBLIOGRAPHY

Colón, Fernando. *The Life of the Admiral Christopher Columbus by his son, Ferdinand.* Translated and annotated by Benjamin Keen. New Brunswick, NJ: Rutgers University Press, 1958.

Fernández-Armesto, Felipe. *Columbus.* New York: Oxford University Press, 1991.

Koning, Hans. *Columbus: His Enterprise.* New York: Monthly Review Press, 1975.

Konstam, Angus. *Historical Atlas of Exploration, 1492–1600.* New York: Checkmark Books, 2000.

Meltzer, Milton. *Columbus and the World Around Him.* New York: Franklin Watts, 1990.

Stavans, Ilan. *Imagining Columbus: The Literary Voyage.* New York: Twayne Publishers, 1993.

INDEX

Acknowledgments

For photographs and artwork: The Art Archive/Mireille Vautier, p. 4; The Art Archive/Naval Museum Genoa/Dagli Orti (A), p. 7; © Bettmann/CORBIS, p. 9; Knights of Columbus Headquarters Museum, pp. 10, 18; Library of Congress, pp. 11, 22, 27; The Art Archive/Bibliothèque Nationale Paris, p. 13; The Art Archive/British Library, p. 14; © North Wind Picture Archives, pp. 16, 17, 23, 24, 25, 31, 32, 36, 37, 39, 40; © Foto Marburg/Art Resource, NY, p. 19; © The Newark Museum/Art Resource, NY, p. 29; The Art Archive/Museo Historico Nacional Buenos Aires/Dagli Orti, p. 35; Museo Naval, Madrid, p. 41; Columbus Memorial Library, Organization of American States, p. 42. Front cover, Art Archive/Museum of Modern Art Mexico/Dagli Orti. Back cover, Museo Naval, Madrid.